Cheerios®

COUNT TO 100

by Justine Fontes
Illustrated by Carolyn Croll

SCHOLASTIC INC.

New York Toronto London Auckland Sydney
Mexico City New Delhi Hong Kong Buenos Aires

ISBN 0-439-70341-7

12 11 10 9 8 7 6 5 4 3 2 1   5 6 7 8 9 10/0

Printed in the U.S.A.
First printing, October 2005

Good morning!
1 sun is in the sky.

Count **one**.

Find the ◯.

1

Go outside. See 2 houses.

Count two.

Find the 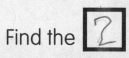 .

How many can you find?

  2

Look up. Find **3** roofs.

Count **three**.

Find the  .

How many can you find?

3

Walk to the store. See 4 cars.

Count **four**. Find the .

How many can you find?

4

There are **5** stores on this street. Stop and shop for a picnic.

Count **five**. Find the 5.

How many can you find?

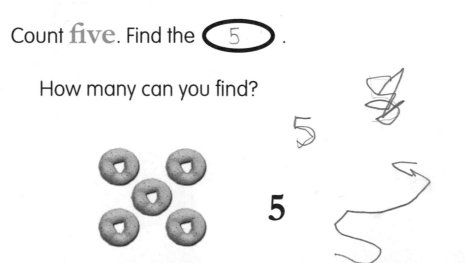

5

5

What should we eat? Buy **6** sandwiches.

Count **six**. Find the  .

How many can you find?

6

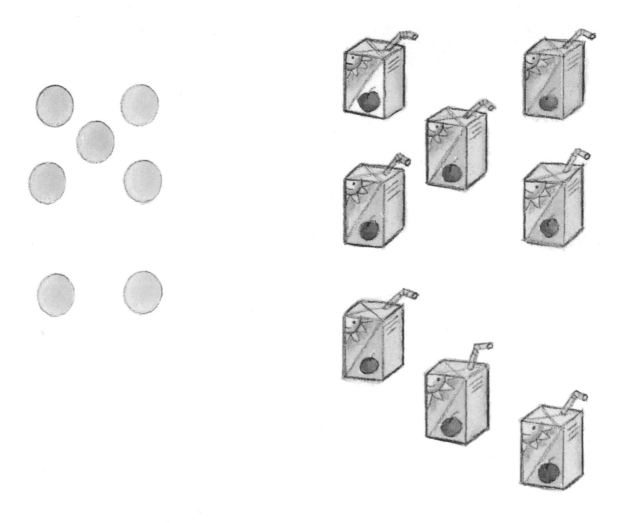

Here are **7** green grapes. They are next to **8** boxes of juice.

Count to **seven**. Then count to **eight**.

Find the ⃝ . Find the ▢ . How many can you find?

7

8

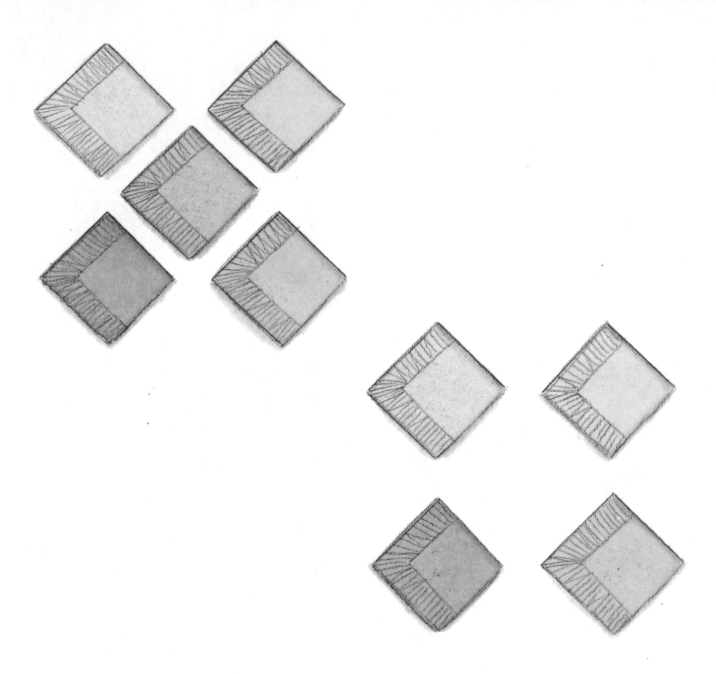

Napkins help keep us clean! Do you see **9**?

Count **nine**. Find the ◇ .

How many can you find?

9

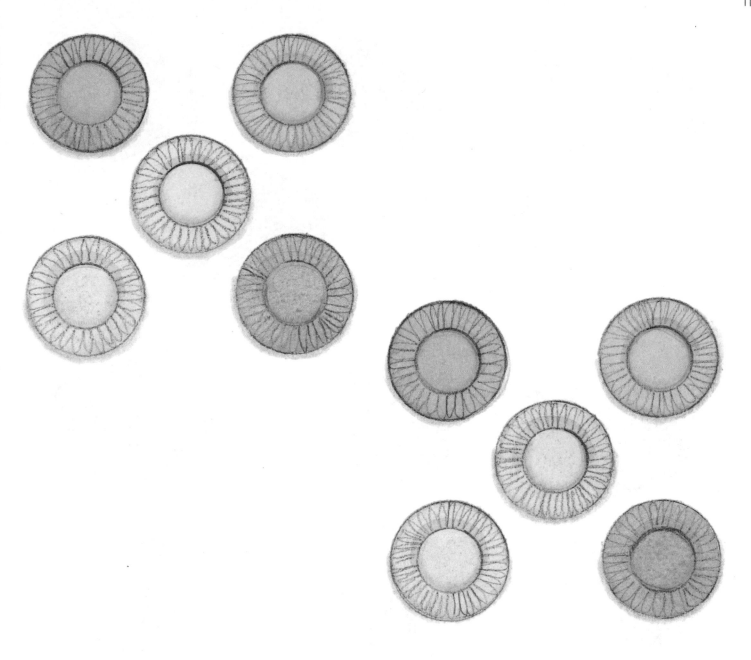

What will we eat our food on? Don't forget **10** paper plates.

Count **ten**. Find the ◯.

How many can you find?

  **10**

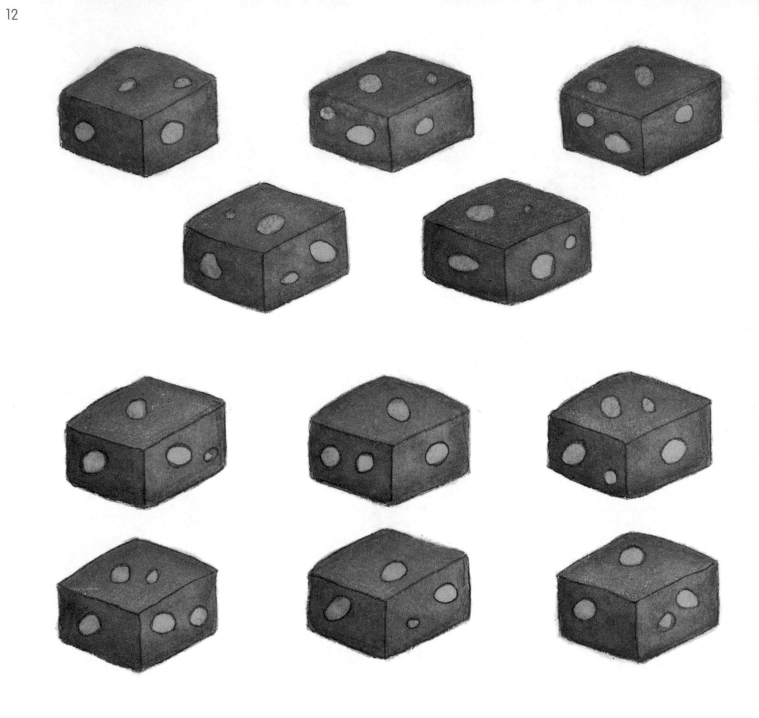

Brownies are yummy, too. Will **11** be enough?

Count **eleven**.

11

Let's pay for lunch. Use 12 coins.

Count twelve.

    **12**

Time to go! Walk 13 stepping stones to the park.

Count **thirteen**.

13

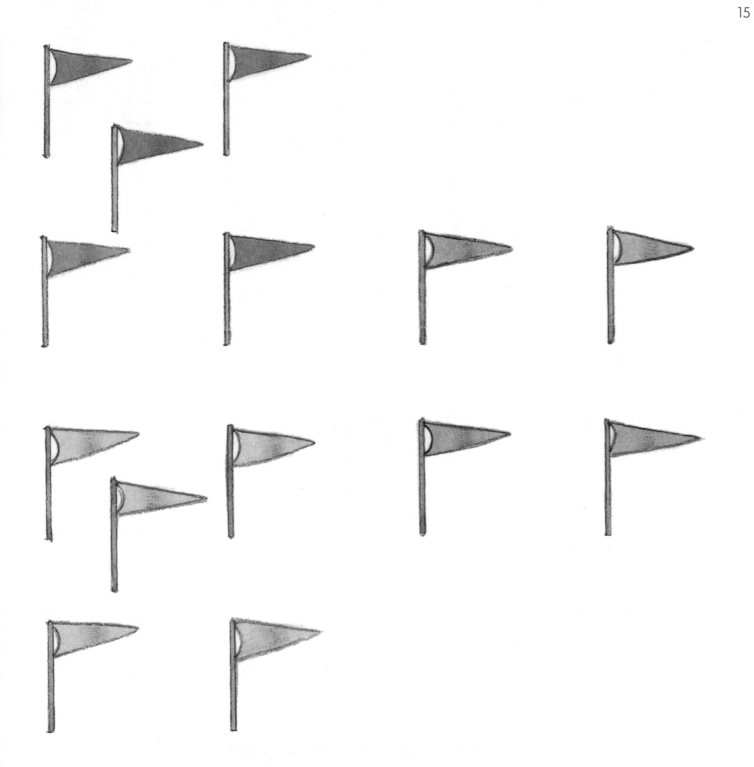

Here we are. 14 flags wave hello.

Count **fourteen**.

14

Let's eat lunch!
Spread 15 blankets on the grass.

Count fifteen.

15

First cut each sandwich in half. Then cut them again.
Now there are **16** squares.

Count **sixteen**.

Look who else is hungry!
17 ants march around the brownie.

Count **seventeen**.

    **17**

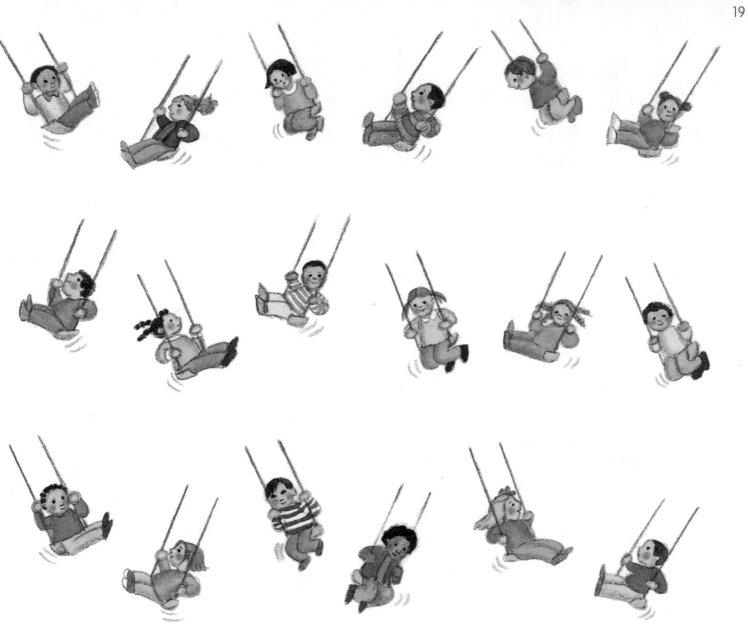

After lunch, it's time to play.
18 swings move back and forth.

Count **eighteen**.

18

19 see-saws go up and down, down and up.

Count **nineteen**.

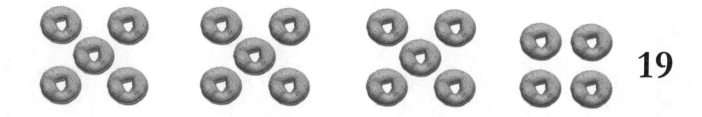

19

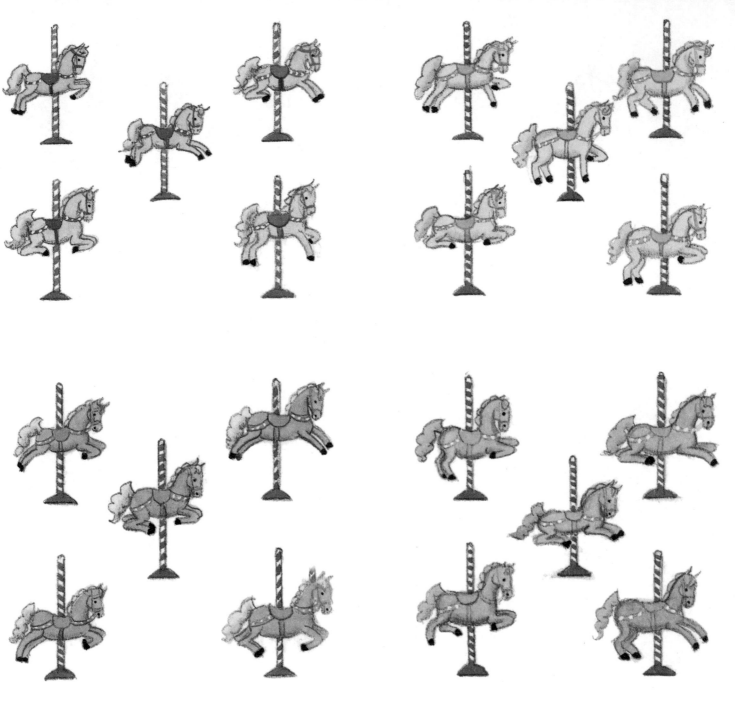

Let's ride on the merry-go-round. 20 horses go round and round.

Count **twenty**.

20

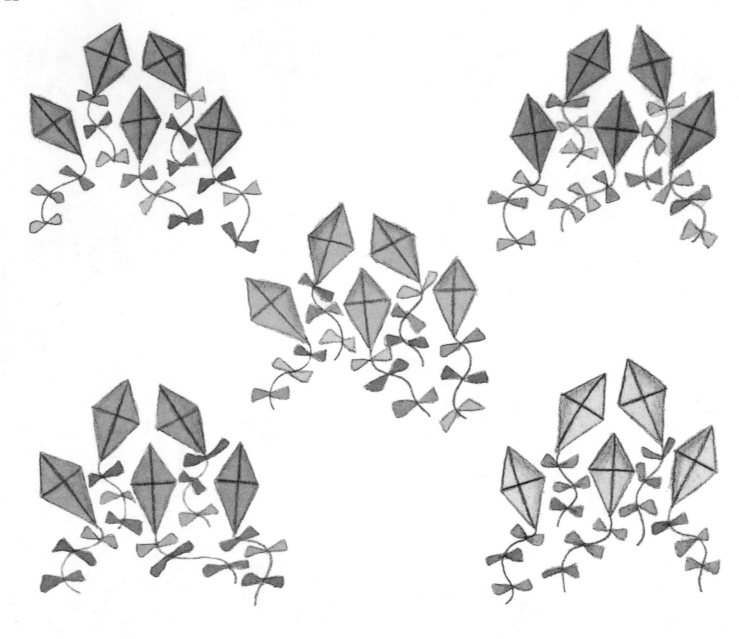

Now let's start to count by 5's. **25** kites fly high.

Count **twenty-five**.

25

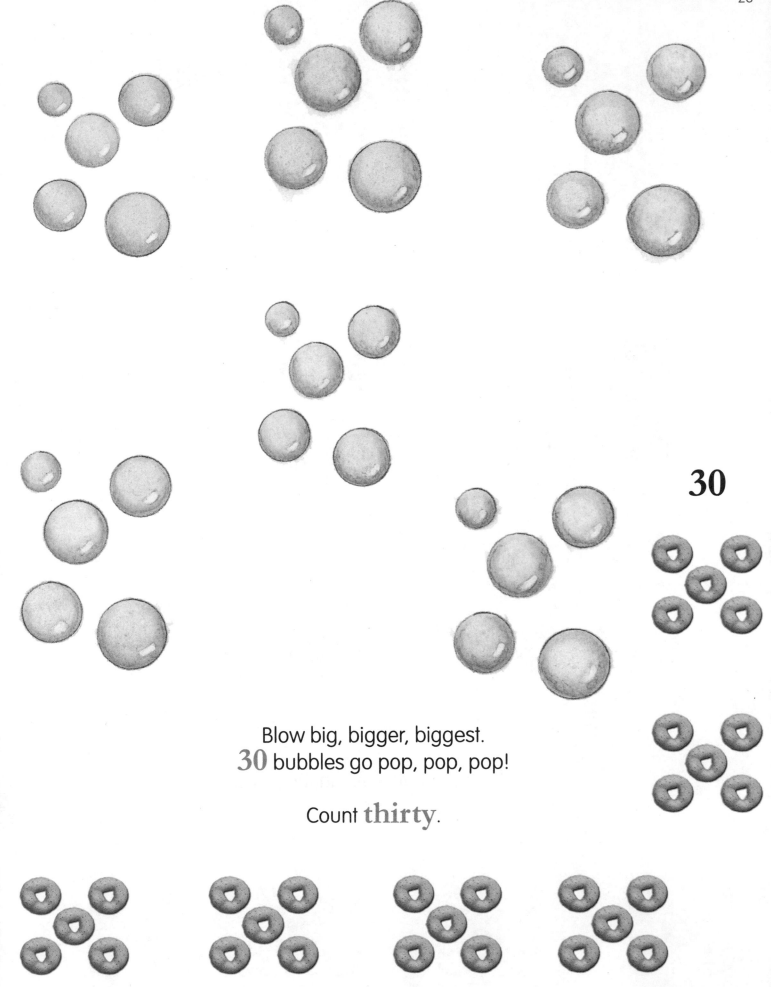

30

Blow big, bigger, biggest.
30 bubbles go pop, pop, pop!

Count **thirty**.

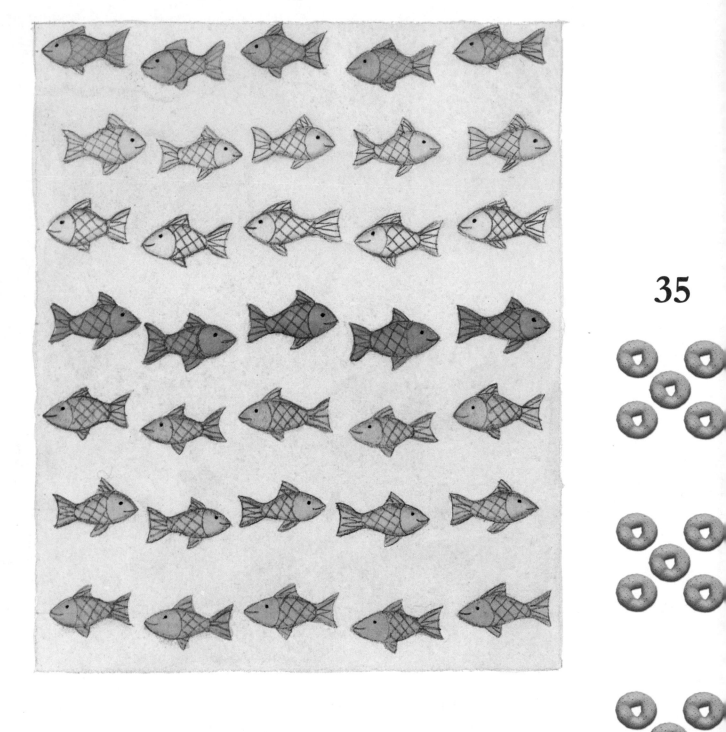

35

35 fish love to swim in the pond.

Count **thirty-five**.

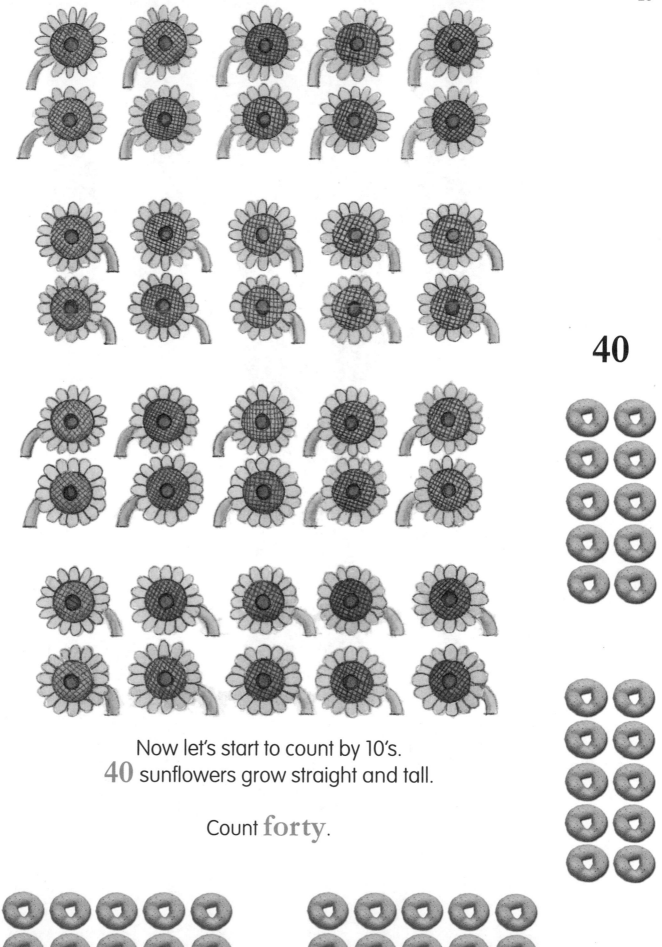

40

Now let's start to count by 10's.
40 sunflowers grow straight and tall.

Count **forty**.

50

Sit under a shady tree with **50** green leaves.

Count **fifty**.

60

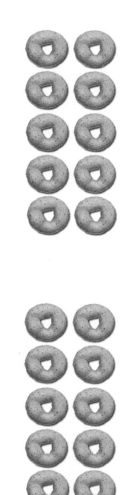

Shh! Don't make a sound.
60 baby birds will soon be hatching.

Count **sixty**.

70

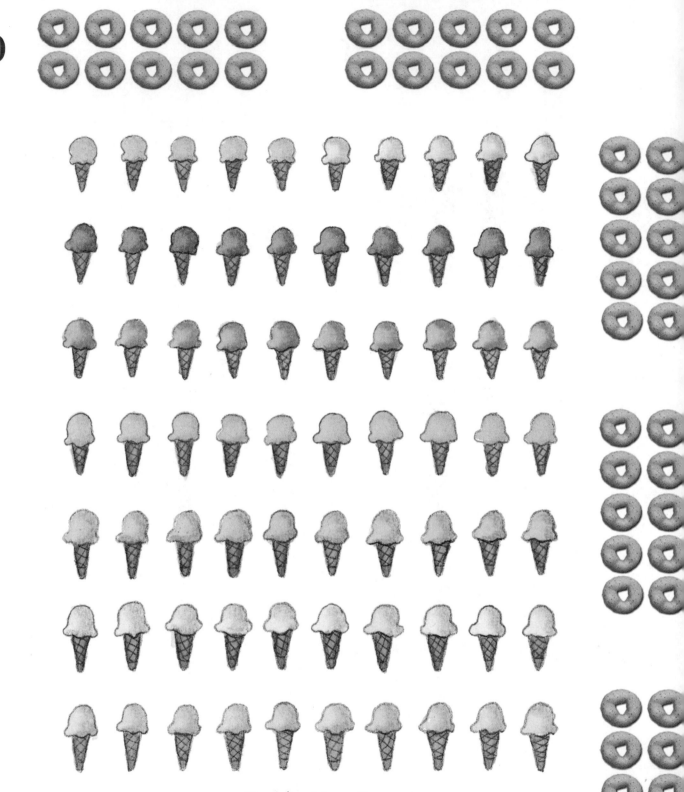

One last treat!
70 ice cream cones ready to eat.

Count **seventy**.

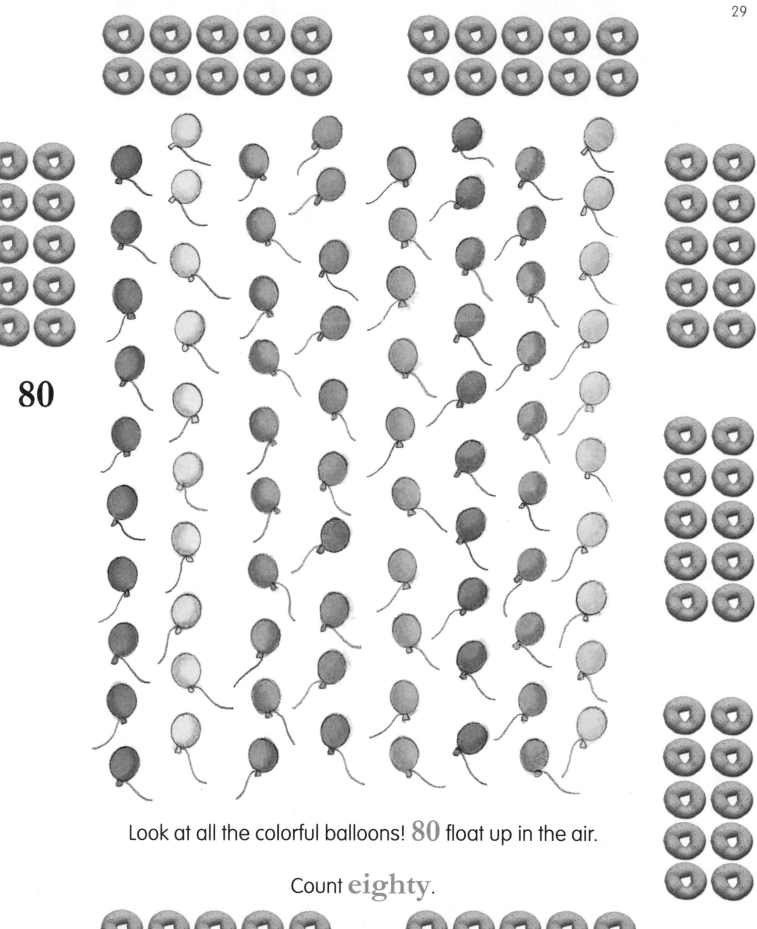

80

Look at all the colorful balloons! **80** float up in the air.

Count **eighty**.

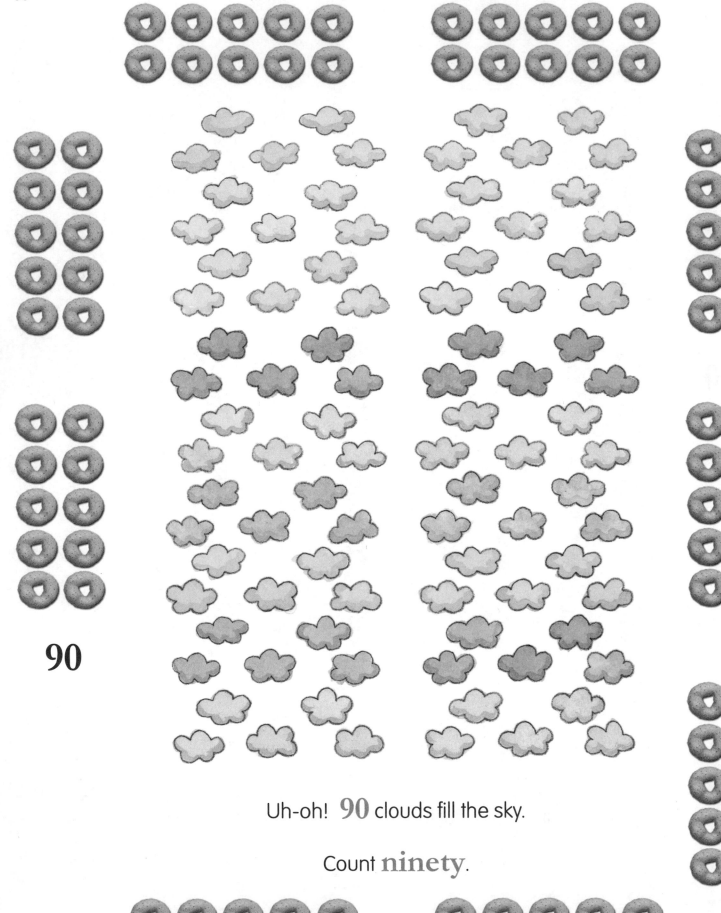

Uh-oh! **90** clouds fill the sky.

Count **ninety**.

90

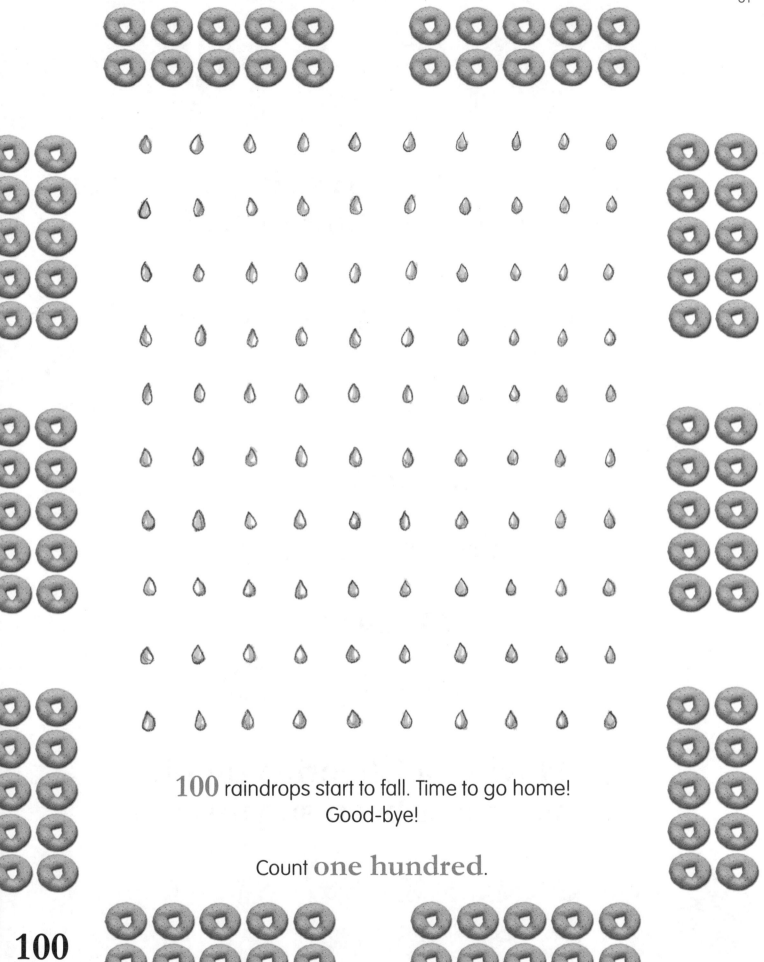

100 raindrops start to fall. Time to go home!
Good-bye!

Count **one hundred**.

100

Did you have fun reading this book
and counting to 100?

Along the way, did you find:

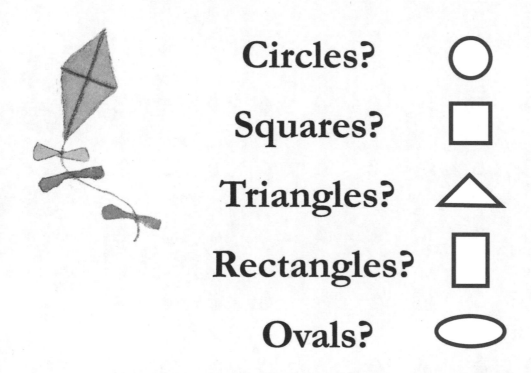

Circles? ○

Squares? □

Triangles? △

Rectangles? ▯

Ovals? ⬭

Having a Cheerios picnic
has never been so yummy!